For all the children of the world . . . and for the sloths
—E.M.

To my brother, Roberto
—B.F.

Visit us on the Web! rhcbooks.com

Educators and librarians, for a variety of teaching tools, visit us at RHTeachersLibrarians.com

Library of Congress Cataloging-in-Publication Data
Names: Muñiz, Emme, author. | Figueroa, Brenda, illustrator.
Title: Lord help me / Emme Muñiz ; illustrator, Brenda Figueroa.
Description: First edition. | New York : Crown Books for Young Readers, 2020. | Audience: Ages 3–7 | Audience: Grades K–1 |
Summary: "The everyday power of prayer comes to life in this inspirational picture book written by
twelve-year-old budding singer Emme Muñiz" —Provided by publisher.
Identifiers: LCCN 2019040721 (print) | LCCN 2019040722 (ebook) | ISBN 978-0-593-12008-8 (hardcover) |
ISBN 978-0-593-12009-5 (library binding) | ISBN 978-0-593-12010-1 (ebook)
Subjects: LCSH: Children—Prayers and devotions—Juvenile literature.
Classification: LCC BV265 .M86 2020 (print) | LCC BV265 (ebook) | DDC 242/.82—dc23

The text of this book is set in 18-point Archer Medium.
The illustrations in this book were created using pencil and ballpoint pen on paper, then colored digitally.

MANUFACTURED IN CHINA
10 9 8 7 6 5 4 3
First Edition

Lord Help Me

Inspiring Prayers for Every Day

Emme Muñiz

Illustrated by Brenda Figueroa

Crown Books for Young Readers

New York

Lord help me to wake up and get out of this warm, cozy bed.

Lord help me to get ready for school on time.

Everything seems so rushed, probably because we are all half asleep.

Lord help me to pay attention in school.

I get distracted easily by friends and classmates.

Lord help me with my homework.

It can be frustrating sometimes because it seems to take so long.

Lord help me to be honest.

I get a funny feeling in my stomach when I fib.

Lord help me to clean my room.

I don't even know how it got this messy.

Lord help me to care for my dog, Lady,
and my bunnies, Nibble and Skittles.

They count on me to feed and brush them,
and I count on them for cuddles and love.

Lord help me to be patient with myself.

I don't do my work as quickly as others, and that's okay.

Lord help me to get along with my brother.

I love having a twin, but we don't always see things the same way.

Lord help me to save the sloths.
They are too slow to save themselves.

TIME TO WALK LADY!

Lord help me to respect the rules. I hear
them in my head, but at times my brain
is thinking of something else.

Lord help me to be more grateful

for all the love and support in my life.

The days can be so busy

that it's easy to forget how blessed I am.

Lord help me to find ways to take care of the world.

We can all do something, no matter how small, to help our planet heal.

Thank you for your love, Jesus. Help me to show love and kindness to others.

Lord help me to fall asleep. Calm my excitement from today and take away all the worries in my head about tomorrow.

Now I lay me down to sleep
I pray the Lord my soul to keep
The angels watch me through the night
Until I wake in the morning light
Help me to do the things I should
To be to others kind and good
In all I do, in all I say
To grow more loving every day
Lord keep me safe this very night
And quiet all my fears
Bless and guard me through the night
Till morning light appears
Amen

Why I Wrote This Book: The Importance of Prayer

I first wrote this book for myself; however, I quickly felt the peace that comes from praying to Jesus about everything that is in my heart. He is more than qualified to handle our wildest dreams and greatest struggles. We can trust Him, even with impossible things. This realization was too profound to keep to myself, so I wanted to publish this book to share my prayers with the world.